THE LIT

CHU

AND

TIPS

ANDREW LANGLEY

THE LITTLE BOOK OF CHUTNEY AND PICKLE TIPS

ANDREW LANGLEY

A.
Absolute Press

First published in Great Britain in 2011 by
Absolute Press
Scarborough House, 29 James Street West
Bath BA1 2BT, England
Phone 44 (0) 1225 316013 **Fax** 44 (0) 1225 445836
E-mail info@absolutepress.co.uk
Web www.absolutepress.co.uk

A catalogue record of this book is available from the British Library

ISBN 13: 9781906650643

Printed and bound in Malta on behalf of Latitude Press

'There was an Old Person of Putney,
Whose food was roast spiders
and chutney'

Edward Lear (1812–1888),
artist and writer of nonsense

1

The fundamental aim of pickling **is to preserve food.** It works because the food – often raw – is immersed in brine or strong acid (that's salty water or vinegar). If these are of the correct strength, they will prevent the growth of the microbes which cause rotting.

2

The term chutney covers an enormous variety of sins.

We usually think of something brown, spicy and vinegary, but it's much more. Chutneys can be wet or dry, sweet or hot, and preserved in a jar or prepared fresh. They can also be made of almost any combination of vegetables, fruits and spices.

3

Store your pickles and chutneys in glass jars.

These should have wide mouths, if possible, which makes it easier to pour in the preserves. The lids should be screwtop and coated with plastic or rubber inside to prevent the vinegar corroding the metal. Kilner jars are perfect.

4

It is vital to **wash and sterilise all jars and bottles before filling them,** to kill off any unwanted microbes inside. One simple way is pop them in a cold oven (lids off) on a baking tray, then heat to about 110°C for 20 minutes. Simpler still, put them in the dishwasher on its hottest setting.

5

You can also sterilise your jars chemically.

Use the kind of sterilising tablets recommended for winemakers. Pop into the jar, dissolve in water and leave for the time specified on the packet. Afterwards, rinse out with clean water – though with delicate flavoured pickles you may still get an aftertaste.

6

Suit your vinegar to your pickle,

and use the best quality you can afford. For strong tastes, such as pickled onions or beetroot, use ordinary malt vinegar. For subtler preparations use cider vinegar or even wine vinegar. Steer well clear of anything which describes itself as 'non-brewed condiment'.

7

Spice up your vinegar. There are many combinations of spices, maybe including whole allspice, cloves, cinnamon, peppercorns and coriander or cardamom seed – develop your own mixtures. Gently bruise the spices and add to the vinegar. Bring to the boil, turn off the heat and leave to steep till cool.

8

For a subtle effect, **flavour wine or cider vinegar with fresh herbs or fruits.** Try tarragon, dill, thyme, hyssop or sage leaves, or fruits such as raspberries or blackberries. No heating here – just steep the flavouring in the vinegar in a cool place for about 5 days before straining and bottling.

9

Pickled onions: stage one.

Even the simplest pickles, such as this old favourite, have two stages. First put the unpeeled onions in a non-reactive vessel and cover with brine – 450g (1lb) of salt to 4 litres (1 gallon) of water. Next day, drain and peel the onions. Then cover them again with fresh brine for 3 days.

10

Pickled onions: stage two.

Drain the onions, rinse them in clean water and dry thoroughly. Pack them into a jar and pour over your prepared vinegar (see 'Tip 7') to cover, retaining the whole spices if you prefer it that way. Seal well and leave for one month.
This basic technique will do for other raw fruit or vegetables.

11

Classic pickles preserve the shape, colour or texture of a food, from eggs and onions to walnuts and gherkins. For this reason, you should **use only healthy, fresh, firm and unspoilt ingredients.**

Anything flabby, wilting or blemished will not make an alluring pickle.

12

Splash out on a high quality preserving pan

– the larger, heavier and more solid the better. It should be made of stainless steel rather than aluminium, copper or iron, which corrode in disturbing ways, and have sturdy handles and a close-fitting lid. A good pan will last you a lifetime of pickling.

13

You need few other

implements and vessels

for chutney-making, but they

must be sturdy and easily washable. Two good-sized sieves, long-handled wooden spoons, squares of muslin for making spice bags, a variety of sharp knives and a big dependable, non-rocking wooden board for chopping and slicing

14

Classic chutneys have several things in common.

One: the ingredients are chopped fairly small. Two: they are cooked slowly over a low heat. And three: the vinegar is sweetened with sugar, producing something halfway between a jam and a pickle.

15

Use your **overgrown, under-ripe, slightly past-it, bruised and ugly produce**

to make chutneys. The same goes for seasonal gluts of stuff like apples and tomatoes. Cunningly mixed and cooked, their faults will fade and they will blend with the other ingredients to create something luscious and intriguing.

16

A pot cover forms a vital barrier between the pickle and the lid. It stops vinegar and salt corroding any exposed metal. When you've filled the jar, pop on a cover before screwing down the lid. Run out of covers? Use greaseproof paper or clingfilm instead.

17

Boiling down chutney is a crucial part of the process.

Too little, and the chutney will be too liquid, and prone to fermentation. Too much, and you may burn it on the bottom of the pan. So simmer it gently – uncovered – for up to 2 hours, stirring occasionally. The chutney is ready when a spoon drawn through it leaves a trail.

18

Here's a basic recipe for tomato chutney.

Adapt it as you will. Cook 1kg (2lb) of red and green tomatoes in 1 litre (2 pints) of vinegar until mushy. Now cook 450g (1lb) of chopped onion, the same of raisins and of brown sugar, plus garlic and chosen spices in 1 litre (2 pints) of vinegar till soft. Combine, reduce for 10 minutes and pot.

19

A wide-mouthed funnel will spare you a lot of mess

when potting hot chutneys and other sloppy preserves. Slot it on top of the jar or pot and ladle the chutney in neatly without dribbling it down the sides. The best material, as before, is stainless steel.

20

Sauerkraut: Stage One.

There's something magical and weird about fermented (as opposed to pickled) cabbage. To start, shred 2 white cabbages and pound to get the juices going. Pack in an earthenware crock with salt mixed in – 25g (1oz) to 1kg (2lb). Put a sterilised wooden board or glass plate on top and weight it down.

21

Sauerkraut Stage Two.

Put the crock in a warm place. Periodically clean and replace the wooden board, and check that the cabbage is submerged. It will bubble away (and pong) for up to 3 weeks. After that, skim and store in a cool place. If kept submerged, the sauerkraut should keep for as long as 3 months.

22

Make sure the fermenting

cabbage

for sauerkraut is kept a good two inches

below the surface of the liquid. This is vital, as it keeps it from spoiling. To weigh down the plate or board, fill a large robust freezer bag with salty water, tie the top and gently settle this on top.

23

Use whole spices in your chutneys and pickles if possible. Whenever you need them, you can grind or crush them. This way, they will retain their **potency and freshness.**

Buy ready-ground spices only if you are going to use them immediately.

24

Screw the lid on as tight as you can. It's easy, with a hot and sticky jar in your hand, just to twist the lid on hurriedly then forget about it. A loose lid can admit the twin threats of oxygen and microbes, and prevent the forming of a slight vacuum inside as the jar cools. Check each lid before storing.

25

Here's a simple apple chutney.

Core 3kg (6lb) of apples (you can use fallers) and chop together with 1.5kg (3lb) of onions and a chunk of ginger. Toast and grind 3 tablespoons of mustard seed. Cook up in the pan with 700g (1.5lb) of brown sugar, 1 litre (2 pints) of vinegar and pinches of salt and cayenne.

26

Tough or fibrous ingredients, such as marrows, parsnips and apples, may **need a little extra cooking time.** Simmer them separately in water for 10 to 20 minutes before draining and adding to the preserving pan.

27

If you’re lucky enough to find green walnuts – pickle ’em.

Cover in salty brine for two weeks, changing the water halfway through. Rinse and dry for a day in the sun (if possible). Pot them up and pour in hot spiced vinegar to cover. Store for a month before eating.

28

Every cook should have a jar of preserved lemons handy.

They add a unique, perky and surprisingly exotic flavour to many dishes, especially tagines, pilaffs, beans and fish. If they're home-made, remove the flesh then chop the rind roughly and bung in the pot at the last minute.

29

Preserving your own lemons is simple. Slice 6 unwaxed lemons, removing the pips. Spread the slices on a plate, sprinkle with salt, cover and refrigerate for 24 hours. Then layer the slices in a jar with a few bay leaves and any brine left over. Top up with olive oil to cover, seal and leave for 2 weeks.

30

Store jars of chutney and pickle in a cool dark place.

If it's too warm, the preserves may start to ferment – with potentially explosive consequences. And bright sunlight will oxidise and spoil the flavour and colour of the contents.

31

Many chutneys are eaten fresh, the classic being *podina* chutney from India. In a food processor, whizz up 100g (4oz) of mint leaves, a small chopped onion, 3 green chillies (de-seeded), plus grated ginger, salt, sugar, lemon juice and a splash of water. Adjust to your taste. Keep in the fridge for up to a week.

32

Narial chutney features fresh coconut.

Blend 100g (3.5oz) of grated coconut, 125g (4oz) of plain yoghurt, 2 de-seeded green chillies, fresh coriander, salt and a little water. Gently toast a teaspoon of mustard seeds in sesame oil and stir into the mixture. Refrigerate and eat within three days.

33

Successful pickling requires the plainest salt you can find.

Sea salt and other unadulterated versions should be fine. But avoid table salt: it contains added chemicals (such as 'anti-caking' agents) which can discolour your pickles or make the brine unpleasantly cloudy.

34

If possible, make pickling brines out of soft water.

Hard water contains lime, which could react with the salt and lower the strength of the brine. If you live in a hard water area, boil the water first. Let it cool, and then scoop out the water, leaving the limey residue behind.

35

For basic piccalilli,

salt 1.5 g (3lb) of vegetables, including tiny onions, cauliflower florets and chopped courgette, carrot and green beans. Leave overnight, then drain and rinse. Make a sauce of 1 litre (1.5 pts) of vinegar with sugar, flour, garlic, mustard powder and ginger to taste. Simmer the vegetables for 10 minutes and pot up.

36

Before pickling,

check whether your fruit or vegetables are waxed.

Shop-bought produce, notably lemons and apples, have often been treated with a protective coating of wax. This will obviously resist the brines and vinegars, which may ruin the end result. Thoroughly scrub suspect fruit in warm soapy water.

37

A pickled egg is one of the wonders of pub gastronomy.

Easy to make, too. Boil eggs for 10 minutes, then cool and shell them and pack them in a wide-mouthed jar. Pour over some some vinegar which has been simmered with white peppercorns, allspice and bay leaves. Try these eggs with a packet of crisps.

38

For a classic sweet mango chutney, peel, stone and chop 1kg (2lb) of firm mangoes. Salt them. Heat up 300ml ($^{1}/_{2}$ pint) of vinegar and 2 tablespoons of brown sugar. Bung in the mangoes, plus 2 chopped apples, a chopped onion, a mashed garlic clove and some ground ginger. Simmer for 1 hour then bottle.

39

Glaze roast or grilled meats with chutney.

It will add a touch of sweetness (and of course spiciness) to the dish. Mix in a little oil with the chutney and spread it on when the meat is nearly done, so it will caramelise but not burn. This works especially well with lamb or pork.

40

Make sure you **label and date your jars** of pickles and chutneys. It's good to know a) the main ingredients, b) the spiciness and c) how long a jar has been on the shelf. And try to use the older preserves first, so they don't get pushed to the back and forgotten until they're inedible.

41

Here's how the Iranians pickle gherkins. Wash the gherkins, and wash and chop some dill and parsley. Let them dry off. Then mix in a bowl with coriander and nigella seed, and a big pinch of salt. Put into a jar, fill to cover with tarragon vinegar, and seal. Leave for a month before eating.

42

A mountain of overgrown courgettes?

Turn them into chutney. Slice (with skin on) into thumb-sized pieces, discarding the seedy centre. Put 2.5kg (5lb) in the pan with 1kg (2lb) of tomatoes and 3 chopped onions, plus garlic, a handful of sultanas, salt and spices. Cook for 2 hours with 1.5kg (3lb) of sugar and 1 litre (2 pints) of vinegar.

43

Make a superior onion marmalade

to eat with game. Thinly slice 1kg (2lb) of onions and cook in butter for 30 minutes with 200g (7oz) of sugar plus salt and pepper. When nice and soft, add 3 glasses of red wine, 1 of sherry vinegar and a splosh of cassis. Cook gently for another 30 minutes, then pot up.

44

This hot lemon pickle is fiery but approachable.

Toast 1 teaspoon each of mustard and fenugreek seeds. Add tablespoons of cayenne, ground turmeric and asafoetida. Grind and mix with salt. Heat sesame oil in the pan and return the spices, then add 6 sliced lemons. When coated, immediately pot and seal.

45

Kimchi is a Korean version of sauerkraut,

used to perk up plain rice. In a crock, mix sliced leaves of oriental cabbage with chopped garlic, ginger and red chillies, dashes of soy and fish sauce, spring onions and brine to cover. As with sauerkraut, ensure the vegetables are kept submerged. Ready in about 3 weeks.

46

Fresh green olives are inedible. If you have a supply, cure them.

Crack gently with a rolling pin and soak in water for 9 days (changing the water every day). Drain and pack in jars with fennel, orange peel, bay leaves and coriander seed. Top up with brine and seal. Eat in 2 weeks.

47

Pickle a plum for Christmas.

Prick 1kg (2lb) of firm plums all over with a needle. Boil up with $^{1}/_{2}$ litre (1 pint) of cider vinegar, juniper berries, salt, chopped ginger and bay leaves. After about 10 minutes, remove the plums and put them in jars. Dissolve 675g (1.5lb) of sugar in the remaining liquid, then pour in to cover the plums.

48

Fish can be pickled too.

Immerse herring fillets in brine for 30 minutes. Drain, slice thinly and pack in jars. Boil up an equal mixture of white wine and white wine vinegar, plus juniper berries, bay leaves, coriander seeds and peppercorns. Drain and pour this over the fish. Eat within three days.

49

After filling a jar, **always wipe away** the excess chutney which has **spilled** round the lid and down the side. Dried sugary **chutney** will not only make a yukky surface, but may also encourage the growth of mould. A warm damp cloth is all that's needed, once the jars have cooled a little.

50

Be patient.

The longer

you leave your chutneys

to mature,
the better.

Although they are approachable after one month at the earliest, they will go on developing flavour for six – or even a whole year. So make sure you've got a plentiful supply.

Andrew Langley

Andrew Langley is a knowledgeable food and drink writer. Among his formative influences he lists a season picking grapes in Bordeaux, several years of raising sheep and chickens in Wiltshire and two decades drinking his grandmother's tea. He has written books on a number of Scottish and Irish whisky distilleries and is the editor of the highly regarded anthology of the writings of the legendary Victorian chef Alexis Soyer.

THE LITTLE BOOK OF
BARBECUE
TIPS
ANDREW LANGLEY

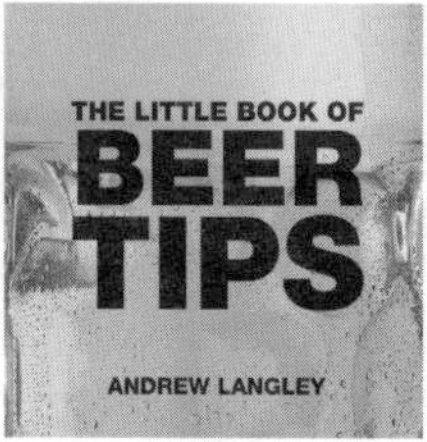
THE LITTLE BOOK OF
BEER
TIPS
ANDREW LANGLEY

THE LITTLE BOOK OF
HERB
TIPS
WILLIAM FORTT

THE LITTLE BOOK OF
POKER
TIPS

THE LITTLE BOOK OF
GARDENING
TIPS
WILLIAM FORTT

THE LITTLE BOOK OF
CHEFS'
TIPS
RICHARD MAGGS

THE LITTLE BOOK OF
SPICE
TIPS
ANDREW LANGLEY

THE LITTLE BOOK OF
GOLF
TIPS
PETER FRENCH

THE LITTLE BOOK OF
TIPS
SERIES

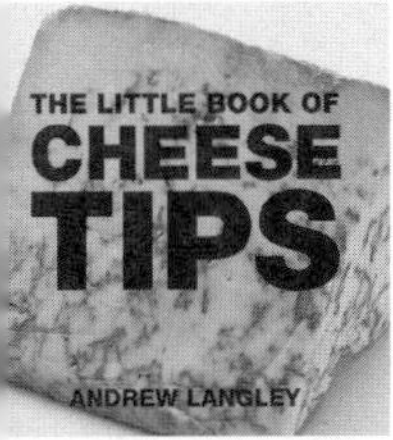
THE LITTLE BOOK OF
CHEESE
TIPS
ANDREW LANGLEY

THE LITTLE BOOK OF
WINE
TIPS
ANDREW LANGLEY

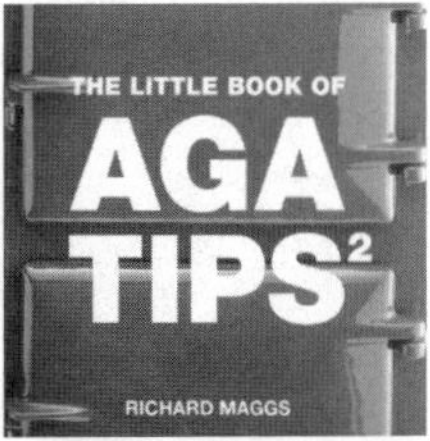
THE LITTLE BOOK OF
AGA
TIPS²
RICHARD MAGGS

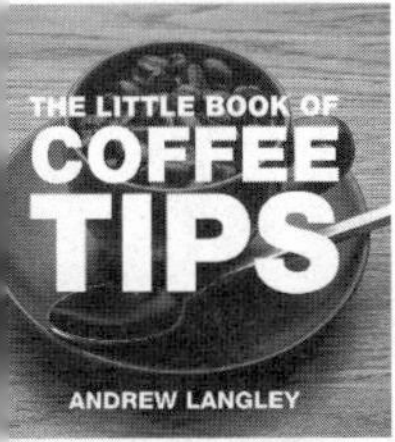
THE LITTLE BOOK OF
COFFEE
TIPS
ANDREW LANGLEY

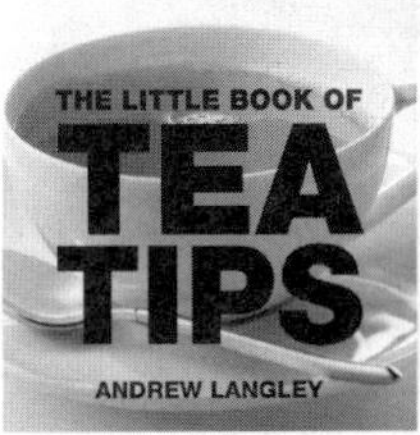
THE LITTLE BOOK OF
TEA
TIPS
ANDREW LANGLEY

THE LITTLE BOOK OF
AGA
TIPS³
RICHARD MAGGS

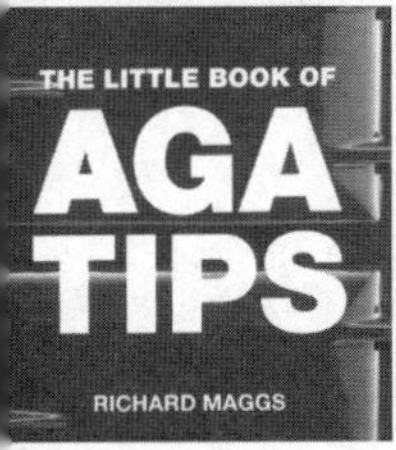
THE LITTLE BOOK OF
AGA
TIPS
RICHARD MAGGS

THE LITTLE BOOK OF
CHRISTMAS
AGA
TIPS
RICHARD MAGGS

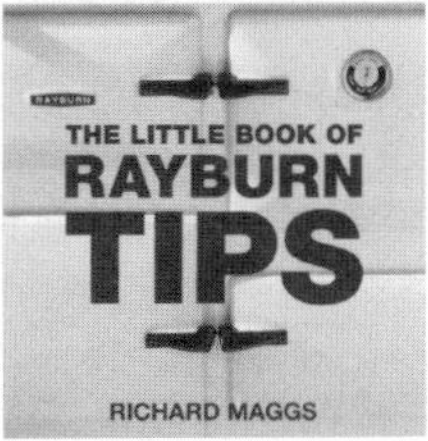
RAYBURN
THE LITTLE BOOK OF
RAYBURN
TIPS
RICHARD MAGGS

THE LITTLE BOOK OF
BRIDGE
TIPS
PETER FRENCH

THE LITTLE BOOK OF
CHESS
TIPS
PETER FRENCH

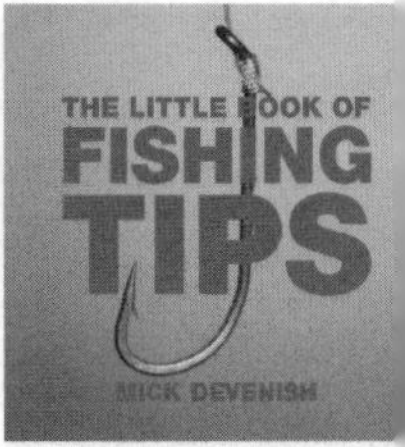
THE LITTLE BOOK OF
FISHING
TIPS
MICK DEVENISH

THE LITTLE BOOK OF
GREEN
TIPS
WILLIAM FORTT

THE LITTLE BOOK OF
KITTEN
TIPS
ANDREW LANGLEY

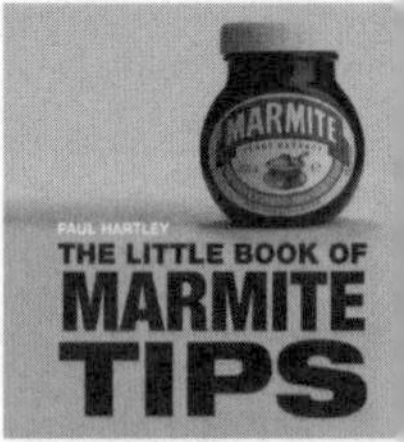
MARMITE
PAUL HARTLEY
THE LITTLE BOOK OF
MARMITE
TIPS

THE LITTLE BOOK OF
PUPPY
TIPS
ANDREW LANGLEY

THE LITTLE BOOK OF
WHISKY
TIPS
ANDREW LANGLEY

THE LITTLE BOOK OF
TRAVEL
TIPS
MEGAN DEVENISH

Little Books of Tips from Absolute Press

Aga Tips
Aga Tips 2
Aga Tips 3
Backgammon Tips
Barbecue Tips
Beer Tips
Bread Tips
Bridge Tips
Cake Decorating Tips
Cheese Tips
Chefs' Tips
Chess Tips
Chocolate Tips
Christmas Aga Tips
Chutney and Pickle Tips
Cocktail Tips
Coffee Tips
Curry Tips
Fishing Tips
Frugal Tips
Gardening Tips
Golf Tips
Green Tips
Grow Your Own Tips
Herb Tips
Houseplant Tips
Jam Tips
Kitten Tips
Macaroon Tips
Marmite Tips
Olive Oil Tips
Pasta Tips
Poker Tips
Puppy Tips
Rayburn Tips
Spice Tips
Tea Tips
Travel Tips
Whisky Tips
Wine Tips
Vinegar Tips